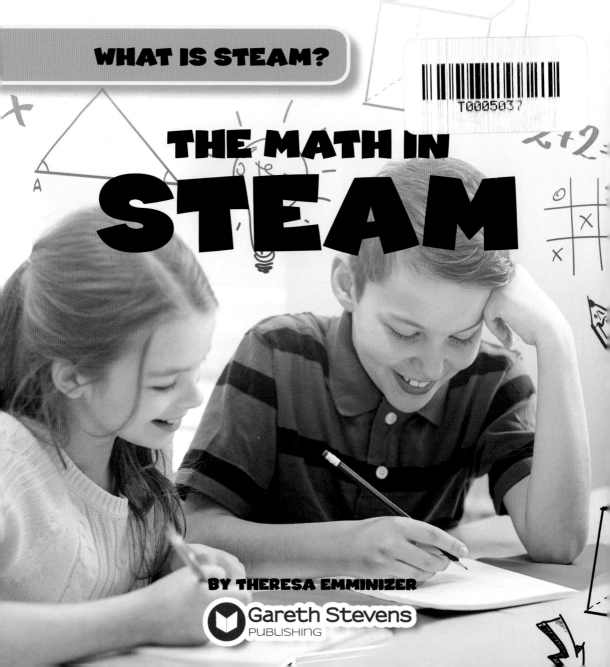

THE MATH IN STEAM

BY THERESA EMMINIZER

Gareth Stevens
PUBLISHING

Please visit our website, www.garethstevens.com. For a free color catalog of all our high-quality books, call toll free 1-800-542-2595 or fax 1-877-542-2596.

Cataloging-in-Publication Data
Names: Emminizer, Theresa.
Title: The math in STEAM / Theresa Emminizer.
Description: New York : Gareth Stevens Publishing, 2024. | Series: What is STEAM? | Includes glossary and index.
Identifiers: ISBN 9781538285503 (pbk.) | ISBN 9781538285510 (library bound) | ISBN 9781538285527 (ebook)
Subjects: LCSH: Mathematics–Juvenile literature. | Mathematicians–Juvenile literature.
Classification: LCC QA40.5 E46 2023 | DDC 510–dc23

Published in 2024 by
Gareth Stevens Publishing
2544 Clinton Street
Buffalo, NY 14224

Designer: Leslie Taylor
Editor: Theresa Emminizer

Photo credits: Series Art (background art) N.Savranska/Shutterstock.com; Cover Ground Picture/Shutterstock.com; p. 5 Rido/Shutterstock.com; p. 7 Sinn P. Photography/Shutterstock.com; p. 9 Evgeny Atamanenko/Shutterstock.com; p. 11 Joyseulay/Shutterstock.com; p. 13 Ground Picture/Shutterstock.com; p. 15 Artmim/Shutterstock.com; p. 17 wavebreakmedia/Shutterstock.com; p. 19 Christin Lola/Shutterstock.com; p. 21 ja-aljona/Shutterstock.com.

Printed in the United States of America

Some of the images in this book illustrate individuals who are models. The depictions do not imply actual situations or events.

CPSIA compliance information: Batch #CSGS24: For further information contact Gareth Stevens at 1-800-542-2595.

Find us on

CONTENTS

Boldface words appear in the glossary.

Studying STEAM

STEAM is short for science, technology, engineering, art, and math. Often, these subjects overlap with one another. All STEAM is about **exploring** and learning about the world. In this book, you'll learn about the math in STEAM.

What Is Math?

Math is the study of numbers. We use math to help us understand the world around us. People who practice math are sometimes called mathematicians. But whether or not they know it, all people use math every day of their lives!

2 + 4 = 6

0 + 3 = 3

3 + 3 = 6

2 + 3 = 5

1 + 1 = 2

0 + 7 = 7

5 + 1 = ____

4 + 3 = ____

1 + 3 = ____

2 + 0 = ____

4 + 1 = ____

3 + 1 = ____

5 + 2 = ____

1 + 0 = ____

2 + 1 = ____

10 + 0 = ____

0 + 9 = ____

6 + 2 = ____

7 + 3 = ____

1 + 3 = ____

7 + 1 = ____

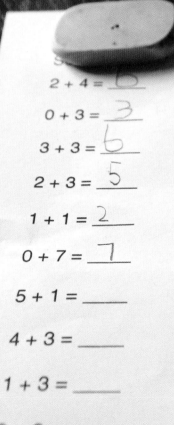

Math All Around Us

Math is everywhere around us. We use math to make food. We use math to play sports. We use math to build buildings, make art, and tell time! Math is one of the most important tools we have.

Mathematicians

Since math is used in so many different ways, mathematicians can work in many different fields. After all, most work that **involves** numbers also involves math! Some mathematicians work in finance, which means they handle money and how it's spent.

Applied Mathematics

Applied mathematics is a way of using math to solve problems in different fields, such as engineering, **physics**, or **computer science**. It means applying, or using, mathematical ideas to look for **patterns** and create, or come up with, new ways of doing things.

Creating Algorithms

An algorithm is a set of steps that's used to solve a problem. In math, algorithms are a bit like **recipes**. You follow the steps to get the answer that you need. Algorithms are often used in computer science.

Making Models

Mathematicians use **models** to study problems and make guesses about what might happen in the **future**. Sometimes these models are used in the health field. A doctor might use a mathematical model to help them diagnose, or figure out what's wrong with someone who is sick!

Math Skills

Being a mathematician is about more than just being good with numbers! Mathematicians need to think creatively. They need to ask questions. Most of all, they need to keep trying. Looking for answers means never giving up.

Are You a Mathematician?

Do you love numbers? Do you think creatively? Do you look for patterns or better ways of doing things? Math can be used in so many different ways to do so many different things! Is math the path for you?

GLOSSARY

computer science: The study of computers.

explore: To search in order to find out new things.

future: What's to come.

involve: To use or have to do with.

model: An example of something.

pattern: The way something happens over and over again.

physics: A branch of science that studies nature, matter, and energy.

recipe: A set of steps to follow to make food.

FOR MORE INFORMATION

BOOKS

Brundle, Joanna. *Classroom to Career: My Job in Math*. New York, NY: PowerKids Press, 2022.

Keppeler, Jill. *STEM Projects in Minecraft: The Unofficial Guide to Using Math in Minecraft*. New York, NY: PowerKids Press, 2020.

WEBSITES

Math Buddies
www.sciencebuddies.org/stem-activities/subjects/pure-mathematics
Try out these fun math activities from Science Buddies!

Math Playground
www.mathplayground.com/
Have fun playing math games!

INDEX